Dear Brian, Roba-r
God's plans are not always
fast, but His ways are always
good. Keep looking into His
loving eyes & keep trusting
His merciful heart.
Love + Prayers
Viv

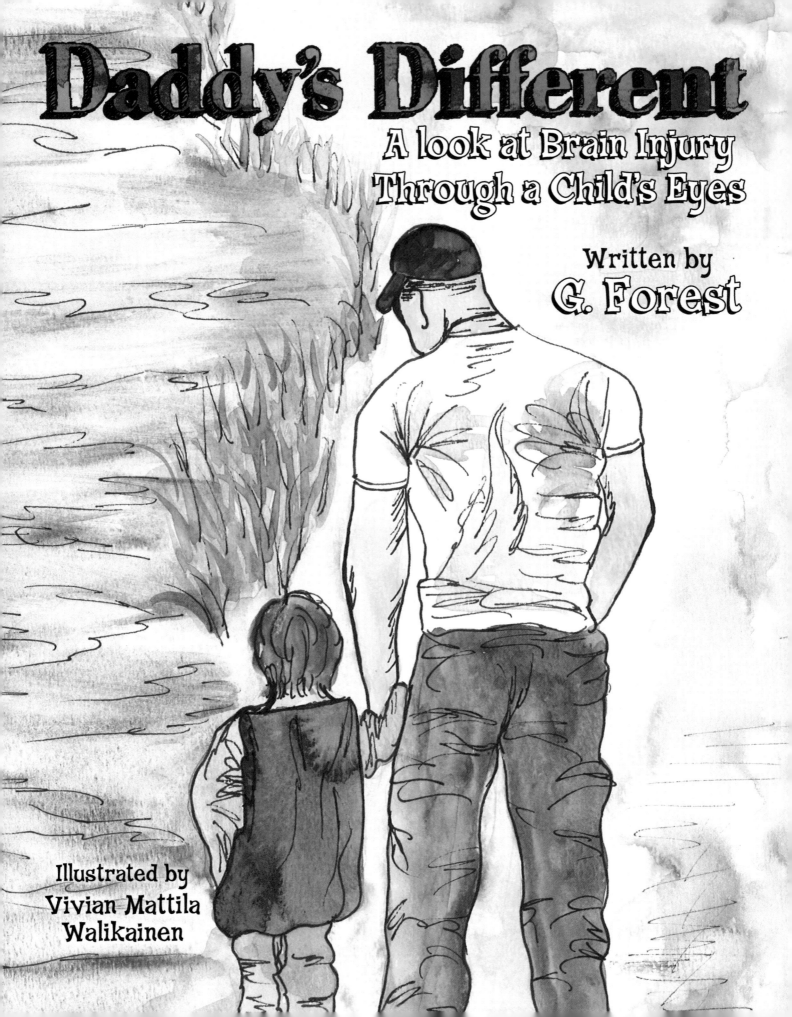

This book is dedicated to:

My parents, Kevin and Melissa Hayden and my second parents,
Ron and Melinda Forest; I wouldn't be here without you.

To my boys, Kaiden and Tristan,

and to my husband, Nathaniel,

whose **heart** has never changed.

-G.F.

To my Children with Love and Prayers.

-V.M.W.

First published by Dog Ear Publishing
4010 W. 86th Street, Ste H
Indianapolis, IN 46268
www.dogearpublishing.net

ISBN: 978-1-4575-1742-6

This book is printed on acid-free paper.

This book is a work of fiction. Places, events, and situations in this book are purely
fictional and any resemblance to actual persons, living or dead, is coincidental.

Printed in the United States of America

Jack was a typical boy who loved lots of things.

He loved learning about animals
and playing games.

He also loved everything about Superheroes.

What Jack loved most of all
though, was his Daddy.

Daddy was his hero.

Jack would tell everyone,

"My Daddy is as strong as an **Elephant**."

"My Daddy is as smart as a **Fox**!"

Sometimes Jack would even say,

"My **Daddy** is as funny as an **Ostrich**,"

because to Jack, Ostriches were

very

funny

birds.

Daddy worked a lot.
But every Saturday,
he would make his
famous,
extra **thick**
Chocolate Chip pancakes for Jack.

He would play Jack's favorite games and

fix Jack's broken toys because

Daddy

could fix anything.

Jack's most favorite thing to do with Daddy
was go for long walks along the river.

They would skip rocks over the water and talk about their dreams.

Jack liked to watch the BIG splashes from the heavy rocks Daddy would throw

into

the

water.

At night, while reading their favorite book together,

Jack would listen to **Daddy's Heart** beat…

Thump… **Thump**

Thump… **Thump**

Daddy would say,

"Do you know what my **Heart** is saying?

It's saying

Jack... **Jack**

Jack... **Jack**

Jack would smile. **Daddy** was his best friend.

One day, when Daddy was away, something happened.

Daddy had an accident and hurt his head.

He stayed away in a hospital for a very long time.

Mommy told Jack,

"Daddy has a **Brain Injury**."

"What's a **brain injury**?" Jack asked.

Mommy said,

"A **brain injury** is when a person hurts the inside of their head where the brain is.

It can be very hard to fix. When **Daddy** comes home, he may not act the same as he used to."

Jack didn't understand.

All he knew was **Daddy** was coming home soon, and that was

the

best

news

in the

world!

When Daddy came home from the hospital, Jack tried to *see* the **brain injury**.

He looked ALL over Daddy's head.

He looked on his forehead, he looked on the top of his head, he even looked behind his ears, but Jack couldn't see it.

Daddy's **brain injury** was *INVISIBLE*.

Mommy tried to explain to Jack,

"You can't see Daddy's **brain injury** because it is inside his head. His brain is going to need time to heal.

Daddy is going to need help with a lot of things

for a while."

After that, Daddy changed.

He started acting different,
but he still looked the same.

Daddy was home a lot. He didn't go to work anymore.

Some days Jack thought

Daddy was as lazy  as a **Lion**.

He would sleep all night and all day too.

Jack would try to play his favorite games with him,

but Daddy was just too tired.

Jack thought **Daddy** didn't want
to spend time with him anymore.
Daddy was acting different,
but he still looked the same.

Sometimes Jack thought **Daddy** was a forgetful **Squirrel**.

He would forget all kinds of things.
Once he forgot Jack's name!
He even forgot how to make his
famous, extra **thick**
Chocolate **C**hip
pancakes.

Jack thought if *he* helped **Daddy** more he would remember.

But he didn't.

Daddy was acting different,

but he still looked the same.

Sometimes Jack thought Daddy was scary,

like a grumpy Grizzly Bear.

He would snap and growl at anyone who dared to get too near.

He even yelled at Jack, something he never did before.

Jack didn't understand

why Daddy

scared him so.

Jack was starting to miss his real **Daddy**.

Some days Daddy wanted quiet, like the Owls of the night.

He would wince at every little noise as if he was in horrible pain. Jack's singing hurt his ears and he wouldn't even *try* to fix Jack's broken car.

Jack began to feel it was his fault Daddy was in pain.

Daddy was acting different,

but he still looked the same.

Some days Daddy seemed more like Daddy, the same
Daddy he remembered.

Daddy would take him back to the river
and they would skip rocks and talk about
their dreams once more.

Jack would hug

his **Daddy** and forget

all about the other animals

he would become.

Daddy wasn't acting

Different.

He was the **Daddy**

Jack remembered.

It was easy for Jack to forget his Daddy's

brain injury.

It was *INVISIBLE* and Jack couldn't see it.

Daddy looked the same.

Mommy said,

"Daddy is trying very hard,

but only TIME will heal his brain."

Waiting for

TIME

to fix Daddy

would

be

hard

for Jack.

No matter how many animals Daddy would become, Jack loved his Daddy and he knew his Daddy still loved him.

Because when Jack would lay his head on Daddy's chest and listen to his Heart it still said

Jack... Jack

Jack... Jack

Daddy's Heart

wasn't different.

Daddy's Heart

was still the same.

CPSIA information can be obtained
at www.ICGtesting.com
Printed in the USA
LVIC051925220513
335112LV00002B

9 781457 517426